When your tummy wobbles and other feelings inside

Ruth Drury

BookLeaf Publishing

Presentation by *BookLeaf Publishing*

Web: www.bookleafpub.com

E-mail: info@bookleafpub.com

ISBN: 9789357695305

First edition 2022

To Mum - You rock

When your tummy wobbles

What to do when your tummy wobbles

Tummies wobble very often
Not only just for food
You sometimes maybe feel this way
When you're in a mood

Tummies get confused you see
you think that you must eat
So you scoff food but not feel better
And stomp round on your feet

You wake up feeling grumpy still
With a wobbly tummy too
Parents tend to send you now
To try and do a poo

But this won't help you either
You still feel wobbly inside
It's feelings that exist in there
They'll do their best to hide

Unhappy feelings like to play
and bring your happy down
They interfere and feel great
If your face shows a frown

Cross feelings feel like pain and make your
tummy sick
But find the right solution, then this can go real
quick

Nervous feelings jump around like giant
jumping beans
They come out of us in different ways -
 they make me act quite mean!

Excited and happy feelings are tricky too you
see
They sometimes get far too big
making trouble for you and me

We need to try some different skills
to help these feelings out
They do not want to cause you pain
Or make you cross and shout

We all have feelings big and small
When we're young or even old
But managing them and staying calm
Is tough to when you're told

So teach yourself these ideas and help your
tummy soothe
Then you'll have strength to face the day,
Calm and in the groove

Tip 1: take deep breaths
Tip 2 : look and name something you can see,
taste, hear, smell and see
Tip 3: remember you are brilliant and everyone
has wobbly tummies sometimes
Tip 4: jump up and down and get some energy
out
Tip 5: grab someone or something you love and
squeeze it right
Tip 6: tell someone about your wobbly tummy
and wonder what it could be wobbling about
Tip 7: eat something crunchy - maybe it is
hungry!
Tip 8: push against something hard and count to
ten at the same time
Tip 9: go to the toilet - this can really help
Tip 10: remember you can do this as you are
fabulous!

Now that you've read these tips and finished this
long list
Go ahead, live your life,
braver knowing this

Your tummy will keep wobbling
It will from time to time
But it's Your tummy and you're in charge
Just like I am with mine.

Sad Days

Sad days

sad days are hard
Sad days are tough
Sad days can come
When you're feeling rough

Sad days mean anger
annoyance and fears
Sad days will often
Involve lots of tears

Sad days can be because of your friends
Sad days can happen when something good ends

Sad days are hard, exhausting and long
They can make you feel like you don't belong

Sad days can come right after some fun
Confusing and strange until the days done

everyone gets these rubbish sad days
And each person deals with them
In their own different ways

Some shout and scream with all of their might
Some people hide in their room until night

Others tell friends and ask for a cuddle
Some will just cry and dissolve in a puddle

Some seek out help from drs and pros
To find inner strength to combat these woes

These different ways won't all work for you
But you'll find your way, I promise it's true

Because
Sad days are hard for everyone
But admitting you're sad
Is one battle won.

All at once

I'm so excited I just can't wait
I'm so worried now what if they're late
I'm really angry, I must not lose
A single game - ooh look my shoes!
I feel quite sick I don't want this
Let's cancel now, give it a miss
Ding dong hooray I'll get the door
They've got a gift, but I want more
I'm nervous that they might hate me
It's scary and I need to pee
I'm happy that I've got a cake
I feel unsure, my smile is fake
I love this day and my friend,
I'm sad that this day has to end
I'll storm off now and not say bye
I'll hide my head and start to cry
I tell my family I'm calm and they
Begin to sing
Happy birthday

Fear

Crash, bang, thump thump thump
Gulp, sigh, bump bump bump
Goes my heart when it feels fear
As though a giant monsters near.

Curious Caterpillar

Caterpillar looking out
Wondering what the worlds about

Why trees are high
And plants are small

Why some bugs fly and
 some just crawl

How flowers grow
And blackbirds sing

And when he'll learn
What is his thing?

Will he grow large and dig up worms
Or will he stay small and only squirm?

How do the clouds stay in the sky
Why do they leak and start to cry?

He asks his dad, sat on a tree
If he could explain curiosity

My little brain just needs to know
About this world and how I'll grow

His dad smiles and then explains
That questions help to grow our brains

They create a passion, deep inside
One which you must never hide

To learn a lot is good for you
It's can be really tiring too

But it leads to so much fun
So go ask questions in the sun

So caterpillar turns around
And climbs right down to the ground

But then he turns around to say
What bug am I? by the way.

The day I died

The day I died

Where did I go?

Did I go to heaven, up in the skies above?
Or am I still beside you,
Unseen but full of love?

Or is my journey over
While yours just keeps on going?
Or am I in the after life, like history books are
showing?

I climbed up high,sat down and then,
I began to think
It all started to make sense,
so gave my dad a wink

He loved me really oh so much
We always had such fun
He played with me and taught me tricks
And let me out to run

I always liked to climb up high
right to my happy place
My favourite spot to be you know,
Was cuddled by your face.

My humans took my body
And placed it in a pot
They wrapped me up nice and warm
Like when you're in a cot

I left my family that day
But never left their heart
They talk about me every day
Like we never were apart

So that's the tale of Maudey
A skinny little rat
Who left this earth, filled up with love
And nothing will change that.

A Nervous Haiku

Nervous worrying
Jitters making feel sick
Deep breath, I got this.

School

Note to adult - please roar like a dinosaur as loud as possible when reading this!

Rahhhhhhhhhhhh

Baby Dino went to school
He thought he'd find it really cool
But he was scared and full of fear
So then rolled down a little tear

Rahhhhhhhhhhh
'Wow Dino, you are cross
Can I help you?' Said the boss
Rah said Dino, leave me be
I'm the one who can help me

Rahhhhhhhhhh

It's all too much
I hate this place
More tears were rolling
down his face

Rahhhhhhhhhh

I wonder if Dino feels quite mad

Or maybe inside he is sad
Maybe missing home or a friend
Or waiting for the day to end
Rahhh

Sobbed Dino
My brain is spinning
My angry voice is sadly winning

Rahhhh

The boss sat down and shared a smile
It's ok Dino, rest a while
We know it's tough to be here
And face up to your biggest fear

Things are new and not the same
So don't think you're the one to blame
We can be scared or stand up proud
And shout this out now really loud

I am Dino and I'm me
So I can't wait for you to see
My braver side when Im able
So come sit here, on my table

Rah

I feel better, not so sad

Infact I'm Feeling really glad
Thanks for helping me to see
My Dino roar can stay in me

Friends - an acrostic

Friends make the day go fast
Real good fun built to last
I wish we'd be pals forever
Even if we don't stay together
Never forgetting our playful times
Discussing love and childhood crimes
Silly, happy and perfect for me.

Anger

Angry angry every day
I get angry when you say
What is wrong?
Or clean this mess
Or sit up straight
Or please don't stress

My anger gets the best of me
No matter if I'm not moody
If my brain simply feels bad
I'll say mean things
And get quite mad

I don't mean it
I'm trying my best
To stay so calm
And not protest

I will get there
I will calm down
And stop my face
Showing a frown

Right now's not good
But soon you'll see
That things change quickly
Inside me

I'll feel better and happy be
So please just stay
 patient with me

There was was a young man
who was sad

There was a young man who was sad
He thought he was exceptionally bad
But he saved someone's life
Then made her his wife
And now he's exceptionally glad

Friends no longer

I don't know why we can't be friends
Arguing, angry, the hurt never ends
We used to laugh and play together
I never knew it wouldn't be forever
I said mean things when I felt sad
You screamed at me and looked so mad
You won't answer now or chat to me
It seems so minor, quite silly
I can't remember what went wrong
Or if we felt this all along
Were we meant to be a team?
Or was it just a wishful dream
I'm sorry for my part in this
I know it's you that I miss
I hope you miss me too my friend
And that this sadness soon will end

- note to reader. Friends are a tricky thing, don't worry if you break friends, you can sort it out when things are calmer. Deep breaths. You got this.

Feelings

To the tune of Twinkle Twinkle Little Star

Feelings are so really tough
They can make things feel quite rough
They muddle up
And mix around
They bring you up
Then to the ground
Feelings are so really tough
They can make things seem quite rough

Happiness is great to feel
It can make things seem unreal
Sadness too, is a funny thing
Up and down like on a swing
Happiness is great to feel
It can make things seem unreal

Mixed up tummies are the worst
You don't know what you feel first
So tell an adult
Tell a friend
Help the muddle quickly end
Mixed up tummies are the worst
You don't know what you feel first

New things

It's all new

New house
New room
New place to keep the broom

New bed
New doors
New looking wooden floors

New teacher
New school
New friends to think I'm cool

New feelings
New fears
New worries to cause some tears

Tell an adult
Tell a friend
Tell a teddy who needs a mend

Calmer tummy
Less tears now
Be really brave and remember how

Happy feels
And friends are great
Do it now, it's not too late

There once were two kids
who were brave

There once were two kids who were brave
Who had a nice dad who's called Dave
They moved into his house,
And they got a pet mouse,
And they tried not to just misbehave

A sonnet of sharing

Sharing is taught worldwide
It shows we love someone
We can give and we can take
Because we love inside
Sharing meals, secrets, things, toys, time, fears,
hopes and dreams
All because we love
Love our family, our friends, our school, our
community, our world, ourselves
We share because we love
Love is known worldwide
It teaches us to share
We must learn to share the world
And show the world we care

On the carpet

On the carpet
We all sit down nicely
And fold our arms quite smart
And listen really carefully
Until we hear a fart

Someone starts to giggle
We turn around and smile
Don't worry, it is healthy to
Let them out
 once in a while

Your body needs to do this
It keeps a healthy you
Don't be embarrassed or ashamed
Your teacher does them too!

Jealousy

Who's that there
Why've they got that?
It should be mine
Look where she's sat!

Why have they come
To ruin my life?
Or does she want
To simply cause me strife?

She's crying now
See all that fuss
I don't do that
Maybe I must.

The cuddles she gets
And lots of new toys
She can't take that
That belongs to us boys

Just me and her
She's kicking her feet
I'll take a look
She does seem quite sweet

She smiles at me
It doesn't make me mad
Maybe she's nice
And not quite that bad

Babies seem a bit ok
I guess they can be fun
So maybe don't panic
If your house gets one.

Hurt

You hurt me
I hurt you
Being hurt makes me feel blue
A real sorry and a friendly smile to you
I feel better,
So do you

Families

Families are lovely things
But can be hard for some
Maybe those who live in care,
no longer seeing mum

Or those who've moved from far away
Not sure now who they are
From this country or from that one
Now living in their car

Families can be cross and shouty
Where sadness is quite strong
When things aren't working out that well
And family life's gone wrong

Unlucky folk who live like that
Aren't bad or mad or mean
Just simply having some struggles
Which maybe stay unseen

So look now at your family
And love just what is there
Whether it is large or small
Or mum or dad aren't there

Families are a tricky thing
so be the one to show
Just how much love can do
And let the kindness flow